Clever Crafts with GLASS JARS

by Chelsey Luciow

raintree
a Capstone company — publishers for children

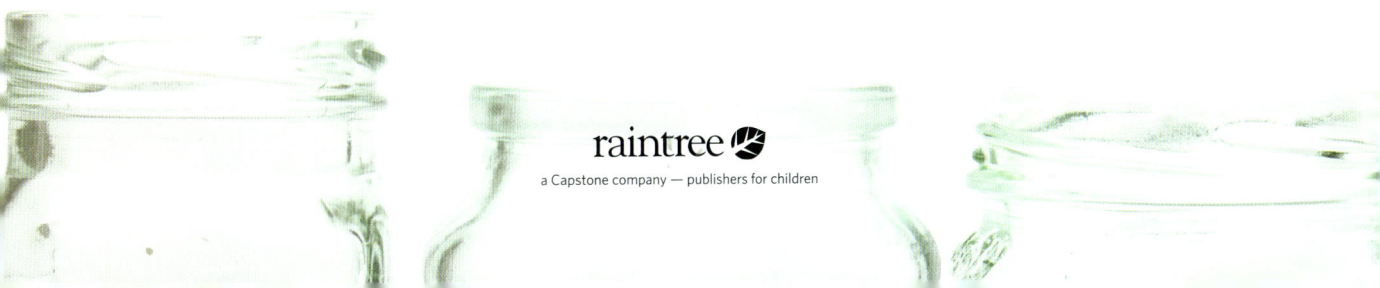

Raintree is an imprint of Capstone Global Library Limited, a company incorporated in England and Wales having its registered office at 264 Banbury Road, Oxford, OX2 7DY – Registered company number: 6695582

www.raintree.co.uk
myorders@raintree.co.uk

Text © Capstone Global Library Limited 2025
The moral rights of the proprietor have been asserted.

All rights reserved. No part of this publication may be reproduced in any form or by any means (including photocopying or storing it in any medium by electronic means and whether or not transiently or incidentally to some other use of this publication) without the written permission of the copyright owner, except in accordance with the provisions of the Copyright, Designs and Patents Act 1988 or under the terms of a licence issued by the Copyright Licensing Agency, 5th Floor, Shackleton House, 4 Battle Bridge Lane, London SE1 2HX (www.cla.co.uk). Applications for the copyright owner's written permission should be addressed to the publisher.

Edited by Jessica Rusick
Designed by Denise Hamernik
Original illustrations © Capstone Global Library Limited 2025
Originated by Capstone Global Library Ltd

978 1 3982 5994 2

British Library Cataloguing in Publication Data
A full catalogue record for this book is available from the British Library.

Acknowledgements
We would like to thank the following for permission to reproduce photographs: Adobe Stock: royalspirit, 4, sommai, 20 (cookies); Mighty Media, Inc.: project photos; Shutterstock: Tiger Images, 23 (stones). Design elements: Adobe Stock: chones, mspoint, Silkstock.

Every effort has been made to contact copyright holders of material reproduced in this book. Any omissions will be rectified in subsequent printings if notice is given to the publisher.

All the internet addresses (URLs) given in this book were valid at the time of going to press. However, due to the dynamic nature of the internet, some addresses may have changed, or sites may have changed or ceased to exist since publication. While the author and publisher regret any inconvenience this may cause readers, no responsibility for any such changes can be accepted by either the author or the publisher.

All product and company names are trademarks™ or registered® trademarks of their respective holders.

The publisher and the author shall not be liable for any damages allegedly arising from the information in this book, and they specifically disclaim any liability from the use or application of any of the contents of this book.

Printed and bound in India.

Contents

Clever glass jar crafts! 4
Hanging garden 6
Friendship soup 8
Colour collections 10
Dog treat jar 12
Salt art jars 14
Terrific terrariums 16
Art supply rainbow 18
Yum jar 20
Solar lantern 22
Aquarium in a jar 24
Snow scene 26
Trip jar 28
Mini suncatchers 30
    Find out more 32
    About the author 32

Clever GLASS JAR CRAFTS!

Glass jars are not just for storing items. They are the perfect crafting material! With a little creativity, you can turn plain old glass jars into tiny terrariums, holiday keepsakes or beautiful snow globes. Gather glass jars from your home. Then use them to make clever crafts!

All about glass jars

Glass jars come in many sizes, shapes and colours. Mason jars are one common type. These airtight containers are commonly used to store and preserve food. Food items such as sauces, pickles and jams are commonly sold in glass jars.

Basic supplies

- buttons
- card stock
- funnel
- glass jars
- hot-glue gun and glue sticks
- paint and paintbrushes
- pencil
- ruler
- scissors
- tweezers

Crafting tips

1. Get ready. Gather all the supplies and read through the instructions carefully before starting a project. Cover your workspace with newspaper or plastic to protect it from messes.

2. Ask first. Get permission to use any supplies you find.

3. Stay safe. Ask an adult for help using hot or sharp tools.

4. Be creative. Project steps are only a guide. Use different materials or try new things to make the project your own!

5. Tidy up. Clean your space once you've finished crafting. Put supplies back where you found them and wipe down your crafting surface.

HANGING GARDEN

Brighten up a wall with this jar garden!

SUPPLIES

- 3 or more small glass jars
- string
- scissors
- ruler
- wooden dowel
- water
- plant cuttings that can survive in water, such as coleus or rosemary

1. Cut a piece of string about 90 centimetres long. Wrap the string once around the jar's neck and tie a knot. Wrap the string around the jar's neck again and tie a double knot. Both ends of the string should be about the same length.

2. Double knot both ends of the string together at the bottom.

3. Loop both ends of the string over the wooden dowel. Pull the jar down through the loop to secure it to the dowel.

4. Repeat steps 1 to 3 with the remaining jars.

5. Cut another length of string about 50 cm long for the hanger. Double knot one end to one side of the dowel. Double knot the other end to the other side of the dowel.

6. Fill the jars with water to about two-thirds full. Add the plant cuttings to the jars. Hang the garden on a sunny wall!

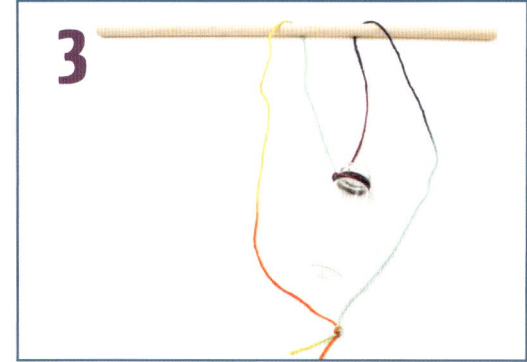

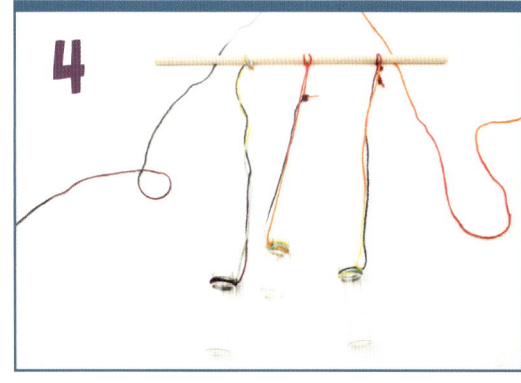

FRIENDSHIP SOUP

INGREDIENTS

- 60 grams coarsely chopped dried onion granules
- 10 g dried mixed herbs
- 80 g chicken or beef bouillon (stock)
- 120 g dried split peas
- 120 g dried green lentils
- 60 g dried red lentils
- 60 g uncooked dried white rice
- 120 g uncooked dried pasta, such as macaroni

Send love and warmth to a loved one using this delicious recipe.

SUPPLIES

- measuring cups and spoons/scales
- large, washed jar with lid
- funnel
- freezer bag
- card stock
- marker pens
- felt-tip pens
- hole punch
- ribbon or string

1. Use the funnel to pour the onion granules, dried herbs and bouillon into the jar. Add the split peas, lentils and rice.

2. Wrap the pasta in a freezer bag. Then add the wrapped pasta on top of the other ingredients in the jar. The bag will keep the pasta from mixing with the other ingredients. Put the lid on the jar to close it.

3. Fold a piece of card stock into a greetings card shape.

4. Write "Friendship Soup" on the card's cover. On one half of the inside, write the ingredients that will need to be added to the soup mix: *500 g cooked and drained minced beef, one 400 g tin of chopped tomatoes, 200 g tomato passata, 2.8 litres water and two cloves chopped garlic.*

5. Write the directions to make the soup on the other half of the card: *Take out the dried pasta and set it aside. Add the soup mix to a large pan with the minced beef, chopped tomatoes, passata, water and garlic. Bring the soup mix to a boil and reduce the heat to low. Cover the pan with a lid and simmer for 50 to 60 minutes, stirring occasionally. Then add the pasta and cook for 10 to 15 more minutes or until the pasta is tender.*

6. Punch a hole in the card's upper-left corner. Use a string or ribbon to loop through the hole and pull the ends through the loop. Tie the card to the neck of the jar.

COLOUR COLLECTIONS

SUPPLIES

- buttons in multiple colours
- items in multiple colours, such as pom-poms, erasers, figurines and art supplies
- small jars with lids
- sandpaper
- acrylic paint and paintbrushes
- hot-glue gun and glue sticks
- paper
- felt-tip pen

A beautiful way to display with a twist for play!

1. Arrange the buttons and items by colour.

2. Sand down the jar lids. This will help the paint stick to the lids better. Once they have been sanded, paint each lid for the colour of collections you have. Let the lids dry.

3. Carefully arrange the items inside each jar. Slide items you want to see along the inside walls of the jars.

4. Hot-glue the buttons on top of each lid.

5. If you would like to make this into an activity, empty out one of the jars and make a list of several items inside. Then hide the items around the room and ask someone to find everything on the list!

DOG TREAT JAR

SUPPLIES

- jar with lid
- pliers
- dog figurine
- hot-glue gun and glue sticks
- spray paint
- patterned paper
- ruler
- black marker pen
- card stock
- stickers
- clear packing tape
- dog treats

Keep your pup's treats fresh in this cute jar!

1. Use pliers to scratch the top of the jar lid. This will help the figurine stick.

2. Hot-glue the dog figurine to the lid.

3. Spray paint the lid and dog. Wait for the paint to dry in between coats. Add coats until the lid and dog are completely covered.

4. Measure a piece of patterned paper that is slightly longer than the jar is round. The paper should be about 7.5 to 10 cm long. Use the marker pen, card stock and stickers to create a label on the patterned paper.

5. Cover the label with packing tape to make it easy to wipe clean.

6. Wrap the label around the jar and tape it in place. Fill up the jar with dog treats and screw on the lid. Now the treats will stay fresh!

CLEVER TIP

This can also be easily made into a treat jar for cats or other pets!

SALT ART JARS

SUPPLIES

- one to two 750 g tubs of table salt
- plastic zip-seal freezer bags
- food colouring
- funnel
- spoon
- slim jars with lids
- long stick or wooden skewer (optional)

Use coloured salt to create works of art in a jar!

1. Add about 250 g of salt to a plastic zip-seal bag. Repeat this step for every colour you want to make.

2. Add 1–3 drops of food colouring to each bag and seal them. Gently knead and shake the bags. The salt should stay dry and should not form into clumps. If you'd like a darker colour, add 1–3 more drops of food colouring.

3. Once you have prepared the colours, use a funnel and spoon to scoop one colour of salt into a jar. Repeat with the remaining colours to form layers.

4. If you like, you could use a skewer to push down the inside walls of the jar to create a tie-dye effect. Screw on the lid when the jar is full.

5. Repeat steps 3 and 4 to fill the other jars. Try different patterns and colour combinations!

CLEVER TIP

Try holding the jar at an angle while you add the salt layers. This will create a fun effect.

TERRIFIC TERRARIUMS

SUPPLIES

- small stones
- jars (no lids)
- indoor plant soil
- spoon
- miniature garden decorations such as gnomes, bird baths and animal figurines
- tweezers
- plants (live or artificial)
- small twig
- acorn top
- hot-glue gun and glue sticks

Build tiny gardens inside jars!

1. Place small stones at the bottom of the jars. These will act as drainage for live plants. The weight will also stabilize the jars.

2. Use the spoon to add 5 to 7.5 cm of soil to each jar.

3. Add the pebbles and garden decorations. Make sure you leave room for the plants.

4. Use tweezers to place the plants. If you use live plants, gently push the roots under the soil.

5. Hot-glue the acorn top to the twig to create a garden post. Place the post inside a jar.

6. Your terrariums are ready to display! If they contain live plants, mist the jars weekly and keep them where they will get sunlight.

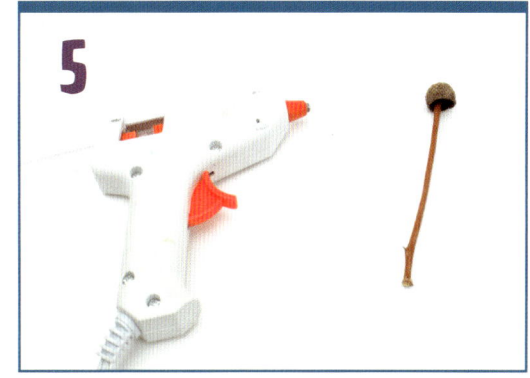

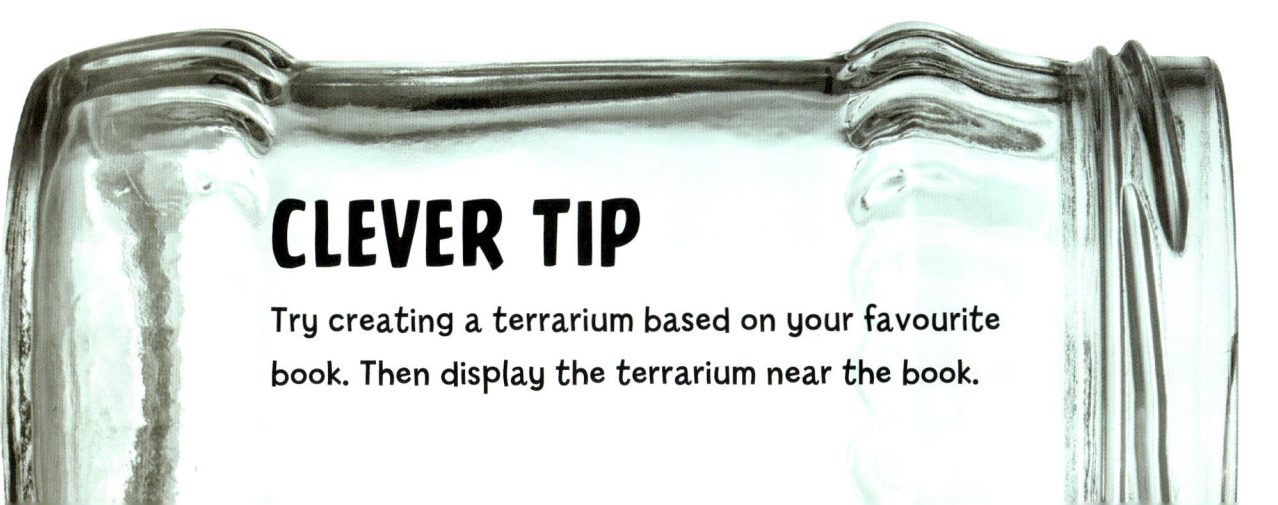

CLEVER TIP

Try creating a terrarium based on your favourite book. Then display the terrarium near the book.

ART SUPPLY RAINBOW

SUPPLIES

- 5 jars of similar size (no lids)
- white spray paint
- acrylic paint and paintbrushes
- art supplies, such as coloured pencils

Paint a rainbow of jars to hold your art supplies!

1. Spray paint the jars. The spray paint will help the acrylic paint stick. Let the jars dry.

2. Paint each jar a different colour. Paint some jars in cool colours, such as green, purple or blue. Paint some jars in warm colours, such as red, yellow or orange. Paint other jars in neutral colours, such as brown or beige. Let the jars dry.

3. Paint designs on each jar. Use cool colours to paint cool-coloured jars. Use warm colours to paint warm-coloured jars. Use neutral colours to paint neutral-coloured jars.

4. Sort the art supplies into cool, warm and neutral colours. Place the supplies in the jar that best matches them. This will help you to find the colour you need!

CLEVER TIP

Use a colour wheel to help decide which colours belong in each jar.

YUM JAR

SUPPLIES
- large jar with lid
- candlestick holder
- hot-glue gun and glue sticks
- gems
- tweezers
- greaseproof paper
- permanent marker pen
- duct tape
- scissors
- sweets and treats

Display your goodies in this fancy jar!

1. Put the jar upside down on a table. Hot-glue the candlestick holder to the bottom of the jar.

2. Hot-glue the gems to the top of the jar's lid. Use tweezers to place the gems.

3. Write a label for the jar, such as "Yum", on greaseproof paper. Cover the writing with coloured duct tape and flip the paper over.

4. On the back of the paper, you will see the label written backwards. Cut out the word.

5. Peel the label from the greaseproof paper and place it on the jar.

6. Wrap the candlestick base in the same colour of duct tape you used for the label. Then fill your jar with treats!

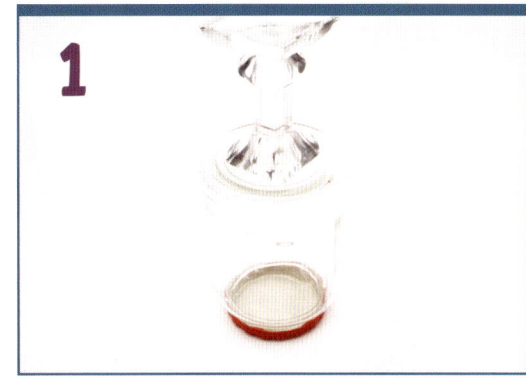

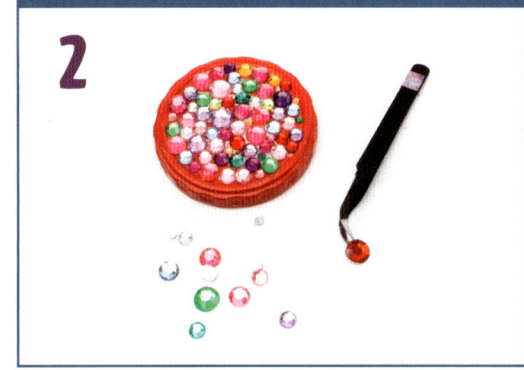

CLEVER TIP

Display your treat jar in the kitchen. Or take it to a sleepover or other event to share!

SOLAR LANTERN

SUPPLIES
- large jar (no lid)
- glass pebbles
- hot-glue gun and glue sticks
- solar light that fits into the jar

Give any space a soft glow with this solar lantern jar!

1. Lay the jar on its side. This will keep the pebbles from sliding off when you begin to glue them on.

2. Place hot glue on the flat side of a pebble. Press the pebble to the jar for several seconds to help it stay in place. Do not apply the pebble to the bottom or rim of the jar. Repeat this step to cover one side of the jar.

3. Carefully turn the jar and repeat step 2 to cover any empty areas.

4. Place the solar light in the jar and let your lantern shine!

CLEVER TIP

Place your solar lantern outside in the Sun to charge. Then use it inside as a nightlight.

AQUARIUM IN A JAR

SUPPLIES

- 480 ml or 500 ml mason jar with lid
- pebbles or aquarium gravel
- decorations such as shells, artificial plants and marine animal figurines
- large measuring jug
- 500 ml water
- blue food colouring
- spoon
- tweezers
- glitter (optional)

No maintenance is required to keep these little jarred aquariums!

1. Place a layer of pebbles or gravel in the bottom of the jar.

2. Add decorations to the jar. If you use plants, weigh them down by nestling them into the rock layer. Place taller decorations towards the back of the scene so everything in the aquarium is visible.

3. Put the water in the measuring jug. Stir one to two drops of food colouring into the water.

4. Slowly pour the blue water into the jar all the way to the top.

5. Check to make sure the decorations have not shifted. If they have, use tweezers to adjust their placement. Sprinkle glitter into the water if you like. Then screw on the lid and enjoy your aquarium!

CLEVER TIP

Want to change your aquarium? Pour the contents through a strainer. Make a new scene, add new blue water and screw on the lid!

SNOW SCENE

SUPPLIES

- scissors
- felt
- animal figurines
- hot-glue gun and glue sticks
- buttons
- miniature fake pine tree
- cotton balls
- glitter

Create a snowy scene with this craft!

1. Cut out small pieces of felt to make winter hats for the animal figurines. Poke holes through the felt to fit over the figurines' ears or heads. Hot-glue the hats to the animals if necessary.

2. Hot-glue two buttons together to make a tree stand. Glue the tree to the stand.

3. Arrange the animals and tree on the inside of the jar lid. Glue them in place.

4. Glue cotton wool balls around the animals and tree for snow. Add more cotton wool balls to the scene to look like snowballs or a snowman.

5. Sprinkle glitter into the empty jar. Carefully screw on the lid. Then flip the jar over to see your snowy scene!

CLEVER TIP

Make a jar for each season! You could add sand to a summer jar or fake flowers to a spring jar.

TRIP JAR

SUPPLIES
- jar with lid
- cardboard
- pencil
- scissors
- pebbles, shells, sand or other material that represents the trip
- drawing supplies and paper (optional)
- hot-glue gun and glue sticks
- long tweezers
- decorations, such as stickers and small toys, that represent the trip
- black pen
- card stock

Remember a wonderful trip by displaying a memory jar in your home!

1. Create a cardboard base for the memory jar by tracing the bottom of the jar and cutting the circle out. Check that the base fits in the bottom of the jar and trim it if necessary.

2. Draw or find images that represent the trip's scenery. Cut them out. Hot-glue the images upright to the base. Cut thin pieces of cardboard to prop up tall cut-outs, such as trees. If you like, you could glue a cut-out around the base's circumference for a background.

3. Place the base into the jar. Add pebbles, shells, sand or another material to keep it in place.

4. Use tweezers to place decorations around the scene. For extra stability, hot-glue the items in place.

5. Write a small label for the trip on card stock and cut it out. Slide the label down the front of the jar and close the lid!

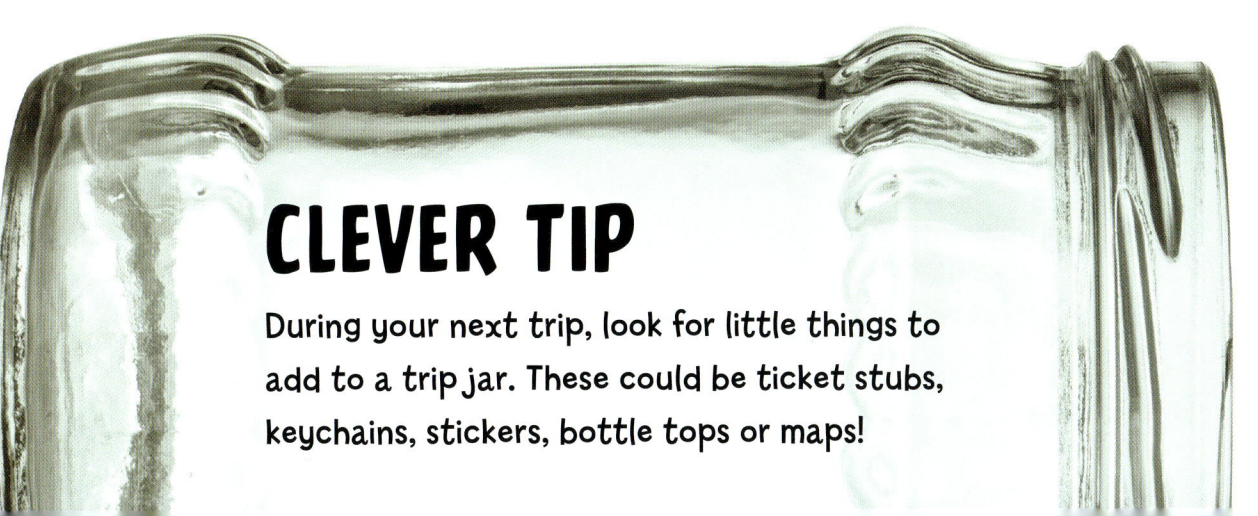

CLEVER TIP

During your next trip, look for little things to add to a trip jar. These could be ticket stubs, keychains, stickers, bottle tops or maps!

MINI SUNCATCHERS

SUPPLIES

- mason jar rubber seals and lids
- white card stock
- pencil
- ruler
- permanent marker pens
- vegetable oil
- small dish
- cotton bud
- scissors
- tape
- string

These little jar-lid suncatchers will light up your day!

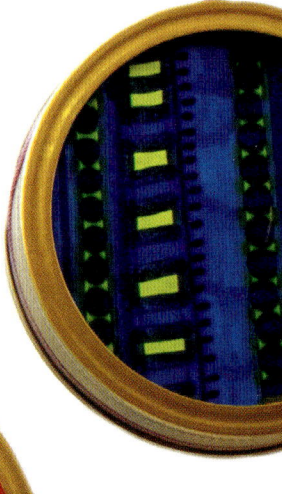

1. Trace the jar bands on the card stock in pencil.

2. Draw designs in the circles in pencil. Use a ruler and the lids to help create different shapes.

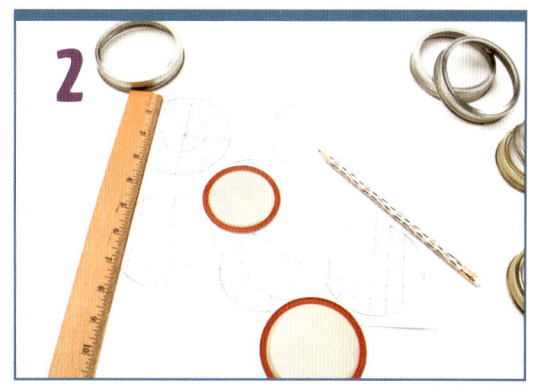

3. Colour in the designs with different colours of permanent marker pen.

4. Pour oil in the dish. Dip the cotton bud into it and colour in the designs with the oil. This will help make the designs transparent in the Sun.

5. Cut out the designs. Tape the designs to the inside of the rings.

6. Wrap a long piece of string around the perimeter of each ring and tie a double knot. The two string ends should be roughly the same length. Double knot the two ends of each string together. Use the strings to hang your suncatchers in a sunny spot!

CLEVER TIP

Frame a personalised message for a loved one! Then give it to them as a gift.

Find out more

Books

10-Minute Crafty Projects (10-Minute Makers), Elsie Olson (Raintree, 2021)

How to Make a Better World, Keilly Swift (DK Children, 2020)

Mini Gifts that Surprise and Delight (Mini Makers), Lauren Kukla (Raintree, 2024)

Websites

www.bakerross.co.uk/craft-ideas/category/grown-ups/themes-grown-ups/jar-craft/
Ask an adult to help you make these glass jar projects.

www.bbc.co.uk/cbbc/thingstodo/bp-kindness-and-worry-jars
Make kindness and worry jars using any spare jars you may have left.

www.romeoandsucculent.co.uk/blog/make-terrarium/
This website gives you instructions on how to make a larger terrarium.

About the author

Chelsey Luciow is an artist and creator. She loves reading with children and believes books are magical. Chelsey lives with her wife, their son and their dogs.